pierre cardin

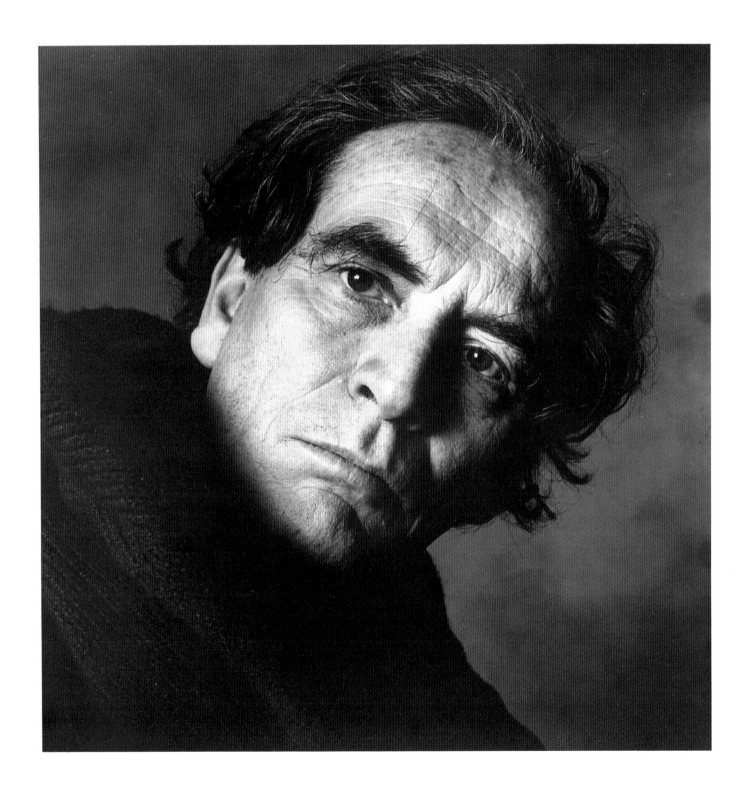

pierre cardin PARIS

past   present   future

with an introductory essay by Valerie Mendes,
Curator of Textiles and Dress at the
Victoria & Albert Museum

Dirk Nishen Publishing
London · Berlin

Acknowledgements

The publishers are grateful to Pierre Cardin for allowing us access to the Cardin photographic archives and for giving of his time, and that of his Paris and London staff as well as to the Victoria & Albert Museum and Valerie Mendes for her written contribution.

We are indebted to the many photographers and publishers who have kindly granted us permission to reproduce their material; particular thanks to Yoshi Takata, Michel Boutefeu, Jean Pierre Masclet, Roland de Vassal, Miyata, Altieri, the International Wool Secretariat, *L'Officiel*, Condé Nast Publications Inc. Despite dilligent enquiries, we regret that it has proved impossible to trace the source of some of the pictures; if omissions and errors have unwittingly been perpetrated, we offer our sincere apologies to those concerned.

Foreword

La Haute Couture est un laboratoire de création qui permet l'étude des formes et des volumes. L'immensité de l'univers et la microscopie cellulaire, les computers et la géométrie sont mes sources d'inspiration. Le vêtement que je préfère est celui que je crée pour le monde de demain.

Haute Couture is a creative laboratory where forms and volumes can be studied. The immensity of the universe and microscopy of the cell, computers and geometry: these are the sources of my inspiration. The garments I prefer are those I create for tomorrow's world.

Pierre Cardin

Pierre Cardin thanks Andre Oliver who has been his Artistic Director since 1952 and who has worked with him in the creation of all his models presented in this catalogue.

Introduction

Haute couture is firmly established at the creative heart of the rich and complex network that forms Pierre Cardin's empire. In spite of diversification, Pierre Cardin remains first and foremost a couturier. To most historians of dress his name is synonymous with imaginatively structured, tailored clothes in which pared down geometric forms and high quality fabrics are united to achieve maximum impact. In the rarified world of high fashion Cardin finds scope for his restless and omniverous talents. While elegant classics have been an essential part of his forty years of design, he has also been an innovative and visionary designer. Ambitiously, he has turned his attention to every aspect of dress though he has occasionally been brought to task for his all-encompassing approach.

Having started designing for women he soon involved himself with men's clothes (1959); children's followed (1966). Not content, as many couturiers, to draw upon the skills of outside accessory designers, he finishes Cardin ensembles with hats, bags, shoes, gloves, stockings, jewellery, watches and even spectacles by Cardin – nothing escapes his attention. With a fiercely loyal, protective and close-knit team Monsieur Cardin directs his activities from headquarters in the Faubourg Saint-Honoré. With his Artistic Director and right hand man, André Oliver he uses the haute couture activities as a laboratory for ideas.

A tailor by training Cardin has complete mastery over the traditional materials of high fashion – luxurious wools, silks, linens and embroideries but he likes nothing better than the challenge of a newly developed man-made fibre. An adventurous and ceaselessly questioning spirit pervades his every move and is clearly apparent in the diversity of the many thousands of couture garments and accessories he has designed since 1950.

After working for short periods in the houses of Paquin and Schiaparelli, Cardin joined Christian Dior in time to make a contribution to the controversial New Look collection of Spring 1947. In 1950 he established his own company and was soon heralded as the new young star of Paris couture. Towards the end of the decade he consolidated his position by producing collections remarkable for their extreme elegance. Press cuttings documenting his 1950s output reveal the Cardin look – streamlined tailored clothes with distinctive details which perfectly match the cool 'hauteur' of 1950s mannequins.

Cardin steadfastly maintains that an ensemble must never be overloaded with ideas, one main concept is sufficient and he has largely adhered to this principle. At the outset he gave certain features his own stamp including asymmetrical necklines, scalloped edges, fan-pleated panels and fastenings of rouleau ties or emphatic buttons. Most of these themes became part of his permanent repertoire but are always re-interpreted to suit the prevailing mood of each particular season.

From 1957 to the present day Cardin has manipulated collars with consummate skill, in the knowledge that a large collar enclosing and focusing attention on an attractive face will almost always prove a dramatic success. 1950s variants included pleated mohair collars so huge that they enclosed the shoulders; deep, stiffened stand-away collars anchored with enormous buttons and, at the end of the decade, a series of exaggerated horseshoe collars which descended from the neck to waistline. Immense, double collars like modern ruffs of padded concentric circles and their sisters of demure white organdie attracted media attention in the 1960s and 1970s and wired platter and funnel collars triumphed in the 1980s. For day wear, a Cardin collar is functional as well as eye catching, being designed to be turned up and protect the owner against inclement weather, but for evening dress, dramatic effect is the primary consideration. In *Paris Fashion* (1972) Serena Sinclair stated "These 'signatures' of the couturiers are fascinating to recognise, for like the motifs on the ruins or the artefacts of an ancient civilisation, they are the instant mark of their taste. Cardin will be known to future archeologists by his giant collars . . ."

Gradually, specific Cardin sculptural 'shapes' were introduced. He made cocoon like coats; engineered pleats and gathers to form looped back jackets and composed concentric oval drapes into unusual skirt fronts. One of his biggest successes in 1954 was the bubble dress, while in 1958 he issued a balloon coat dress pulled into shape by a drawstring threaded through the hem. This was followed by start-ling puff ball panniers in 1960. His 1960 collections were also notable for a group of waistless coats in dramatic colours that were trapeziums in which all details were eliminated save for large matching buttons and extraordinary sugar loaf hats which extended the line eighteen inches above the head. The following year the theme was embellished with drop-waisted voluminous coats whose flare was echoed by souwester-like picture hats with fly away back brims.

By issuing a ready-to-wear collection under licence in 1959 Cardin flouted the laws of the Chambre Syndicale de la Couture and for a period was exiled from membership of this elite group. At about the same time he introduced menswear collections and, being handsome and photogenic, often modelled his own cre-ations. In 1959 *Jardin des Modes* published an interview 'Pierre Cardin nous pro-pose un nouveau dandysme' accompanied by shots of the designer casually dressed in grey flannel tapered trousers without turn ups, a round-necked jacket and knitted sleeveless pullover with low roll-neck. He confessed to being a revolu-tionary in the matter of male fashion wishing to combine elegance with comfort and reject the rigidity of establishment dressing. The collarless, round necked, single breasted Cardin jacket and tapered trousers became world famous when he designed special versions in grey piped with black for the Beatles. The menswear operation went from strength to strength, introducing many new looks which became international currency. To this day, the original aim of uniting ease with elegance is still the ruling factor in the bi-annual menswear shows.

That redoubtable fashion editor Ernestine Carter inaugurated the first Sunday Times Fashion Awards in 1963. A prestigious international jury voted Pierre Car-din the winner of the French award as 'an original designer and one of the few outside the Balenciaga orbit'. It was decided that 'Although many of his collections have been controversial, he remains true to his own inspiration'. Even more provocative collections were in the Cardin pipeline for what remained of the 1960s – collections for which he was to gain enduring recognition.

As early as 1958 Cardin introduced helmet-like felt hats which imparted a streamlined modernist look to his work. He has a purist attitude towards grooming and hairstyling. When his mannequins are bareheaded (usually only in evening wear) they have their hair pulled back severely in classic french chignons like ballet dancers or have sleek, firmly controlled bobbed haircuts resembling helmets. Elegant collections still observing 1950s codes of high fashion mark Cardin's work in the early 1960s but in 1964–5 he broke away from mainstream haute couture and joined the futuristic lobby. This move was to earn him the 'Space Age' label.

Cardin is an indefatigable traveller and visited Japan in 1957 when it was still in the throes of post-war recovery. It is now commonplace for mannequins from varied ethnic origins to grace the catwalks and pages of glossy magazines. This was not the case in 1962 when Cardin brought Hiroko from Tokyo to Paris, there to act as his muse. As Brigid Keenan states in *The Woman We Wanted to Look Like* 'Hiroko, the doll-like Japanese model, was Cardin's favourite in the sixties. She was so tiny that no other model girl could fit into her clothes' and affirmed that Cardin 'made all his best clothes on her'. At the outset Cardin reserved orientally-inspired clothes for this diminutive mannequin but broke the habit to discover that she was the ideal vehicle for his hard-edged, futuristic creations. Hiroko became internationally famous via the fashion press where she was usually photographed in Cardin's most outlandish designs, frequently peeping wistfully through visors in domed helmets.

Cardin used densely-woven, heavy-weight fabrics in a masterly way to achieve clothes that almost stood up by themselves and had clean, sharp lines; lines which were related to contemporary movements in abstract art. Continuing links with the fine arts in 1966, he produced a series of simple shifts that, patterned with targets, diamonds, squares and circles in vibrant colours, resembled artists' canvases. Typically Cardin continued the geometric look by perching rectangular pill boxes on neatly coiffured heads. Textile manufacturers issued luxury fashion fabrics that were works of art in their own right. One spectacular abstract design (1968) employing stripes and circles in fluorescent colours by Ducharne was made into flared shifts which were then photographed on a demolition site.

Each successive Cardin collection was crammed with ideas. He experimented with outfits in boldly-checked wools and continued the huge plaids on matching leggings. All garments were finished by appropriate yet often outrageous headgear. To ring the changes for one ensemble he made an en suite hood which formed a heart-shaped frame around the face.

Like it or not, in the 1960s one could not avoid the space race. Ever since the Russians hurled Yuri Gargarin into orbit in 1961 the media compulsively published, in minute detail, each breakthrough, be it American or Russian and space travel began to pervade the wider cultural scene. It was in 1965 for example, that Stanley Kubrick started filming *2001: A Space Odyssey* which became a cult soon after its release in 1968. Fashion was not immune. Cardin, always preoccu-

pied with futuristic imaginings, was fascinated by the conquest of space and the paraphenalia that accompanied each launch. Interviewed by David Leitch for *The Sunday Times* in 1984, he had no hesitation in pronouncing that his greatest achievement was to have walked in the same space suit that Neil Armstrong wore on the moon. Possibly inspired by the first walk in space by astronaut Major Ed White, Cardin released his Cosmos range in 1966. Every member of the family was accommodated. The basic outfit was practical and unisex consisting of a short tunic or pinafore over body fitting, jersey rib sweater and tights or trousers. A domed felt hat echoing cosmonaut's helmets completed a female Cosmos and a peaked cap resembling NASA off duty attire was worn by men. In fact a Cardin Cosmos was functionally dressed for comfort and mobility but the complete ensemble was far too adventurous for general consumption. However, the pinafore without its space-like accessories was copied by mass manufacturers and rushed into high street shops. Cardin said of his work at this time "The clothes that I prefer are those I invent for a life that doesn't exist yet – the world of tomorrow".

An extension of Cosmocorps resulted in a blatantly youthful collection of spring 1967 including monogrammed (PC) vividly-coloured flared shifts with matching straw helmets and waists wound around with deep cummerbunds in glove leather. *Elle* magazine decided that this collection heralded the 'new boy and girl' and organised an all-night photographic shoot in their studios. The venture involved 70 staff and five photographers who took 3,000 photographs between 6.00pm and 6.00am the next morning. For evening the Cosmos pinafore's hem was dropped and Cardin experimented with different shoulder straps and geometric cutouts. Uncluttered lines in shape maintaining woollen gabardine were set against sequinned, body-hugging undergarments.

As noted earlier, collections of this period were replete with ideas, many of which were too avant garde and their potential was never developed. He released 'Cardine', a synthetic fabric that was given a three-dimensional pattern by a moulding process and created beaded evening dresses with steeply dipping hemlines worn over matching beaded stockings.

Cardin was the first to avoid the unseemly over-exposure of fleshy pink legs (the usual consequence of short skirts) by putting his mannequins in heavy denier coloured tights in cold weather and in dense white or patterned tights in summer. He also introduced thigh length shiny boots for those who were daring enough. When appropriate he still uses the method of streamlining the body in black sweater, tights and close fitting hat as a foil to the main items of clothing.

The ploy of emphasising breasts by protuberant panels or cones is not new. Between 1966 and 1968 Cardin introduced a number of variants. In one group of simple day shifts he inserted stiffened square or round breast panels in matching fabric. More outrageous were silver circles which enlivened a straight black tunic.

Towards the end of the 1960s Cardin made heavy-weight wools with strong checks and stripes into outer garments notable for their powerful forms which ranged from vast swing coats to conical and barrel shaped capes. In addition to relying upon the dense fabrics to retain the required shapes, padded rolled edges helped keep the line.

Cardin recognises the value of simplicity and understatement. His minimalist approach triumphed in the late 1960s when the young and fashionable desired definite, uncluttered clothes and he provided them with garments notable for their purity of line. At the same time he was capable of striking bizarre notes as in a group of deck chair striped body suits teamed with minute tabbed skirts; perspex helmets and plastic torso adornments. Between 1968 and 1970 Cardin's space phobia was at its peak and culminated in his most modernistic creations ranging from silver leather outfits featuring geodesic bonnets to vinyl two-piece bathing suits. Fashion editors had the garments photographed in lunar like landscapes or employed laser lights and clouds of dry ice to suggest unearthly locations.

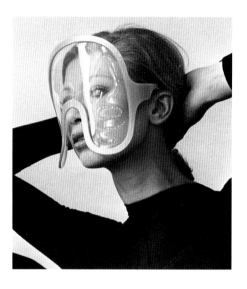

The significant stylistic shift from short minis to calf- and ankle-length garments known as midis and maxis was readily accommodated in the Cardin atelier. Over the customary smoothline body suit minis were put under maxi coats and gave the wearer the best of both worlds. Claude Berthod reported in *Elle*, February 1972 "Qui a eu l'idée le premier de mélanger mini-jupe et maxi-manteau? Cardin". In 1970 clients were offered a choice of outfits decorated with interlocking sinuous motifs in all lengths. Another seductive ploy to solve the changing hemline involved long skirts of broad 'fringes' terminating in circles or pompons. In movement the 'fringes' swirl apart giving tantalising glimpses of the legs. In the early 1970s Cardin continued to apply these paper cut out techniques to fabric which resulted in innumerable narrow panels requiring impeccable facing and finishing by skilled seamstresses. In day-wear, tab skirted jackets were teamed with cut-off trousers, whereas for evening, entire dresses were composed of concentric bands joined only at the shoulders and worn over black or white skin-tight cat suits.

In 1969 Cardin started to design on the mannequin Maryse Gaspard (now Directrice of Haute Couture at L'Hotel de Clermont-Tonnerre). Tall, striking and naturally elegant, she was the ideal vehicle for his inventions. In 1971 she showed a collection of designs in heavy jersey knit off to perfection. Once again it was a collection embodying ideas that were ahead of their time and many of the garments could be worn today and not look dated. Cardin created powerful geometric shapes for tunics, dresses and trouser-suits of pure line and strong detail. Some tunics were virtually rectangles pierced by large circles through which broad patent belts were fastened – sleeves and tunic were cut in one piece. Other sleeves had tabbed extensions floating from the underarms. Dresses had the highest possible choker collars and flared skirts with pointed hems while trousers had globular bottoms slashed over patent chukka boots. The mini/maxi dilemma was also resolved in a compromise skirt which was a straightforward mini on one side; the other side was lengthened to the calf by mobile tabs.

Cardin, created by and creating for the chic and artifice of metropolitan life, found the unkempt ethnic look promoted by the 1970s hippy movement anathema. Not for him the layered cottons of pseudo milk-maid costume. He remained true to his rigorous concepts of form and dress but now in softer fabrics which replaced the solid textiles of the 1960s. A particular favourite throughout the 1970s was single angora jersey with its excellent draping qualities. The circle had long been part of the Cardin repertoire but in the early 1970s he took it one

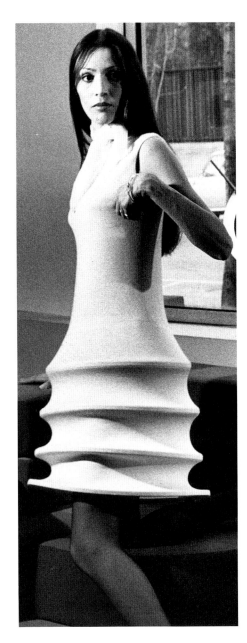

step further and began experiments with hooped dresses. Flared shifts in brightly coloured jersey had their skirts threaded with descending rows of hoops and, if they had sleeves, cuffs were held proud of the wrists by miniature hoops. In the abstract and on the correct pencil-thin model these clothes were most effective but they were hazardous and not easy to wear, so did not gain widespread currency.

Throughout the mid-1970s Cardin draped and gathered fabrics into clothes with flowing lines, and soft loops were an important part of the cut. Fluid skirts worn with skinny sweaters, had side extensions which wrapped over the shoulders. Body-hugging jersey sheath dresses were worn with fly-away capes and ankle-length evening dresses were asymmetrically cut with looped extensions forming one sleeve while the other arm was left bare. About this time Cardin started to utilise bustier and bertha tops above straightline skirts or flared culottes. For summer, bustiers were tiny cropped bands, sometimes shaped and held in place by narrow straps. Bertha tops encircled the torso and upper arms to waist level and in winter were in woollen tweed over roll-necked pullovers. For summer, in lightweight knits the berthas were shorter, leaving shoulders bare and silk skirts billowed from the high waists. Jersey rib bands were used to nip in waists; to form narrow bustiers and in the case of one strapless evening dress delineate the neck and trim a vertically slashed 'pocket' which ran from waist to ankle through which limbs clad in opaque black tights were visible. Knitted fine wools and angoras were cut into a variety of unusual garments including sophisticated *combinasion* and a strange one-legged garment which crossed a dress with trousers. Short tunics were tight into the knees and had huge sleeves with armholes beginning at thigh level. Variations on the jumpsuit theme were given much editorial coverage especially a pierrot like ensemble of black jersey overalls with an enormous pleated double collar in bright red wool. Cardin even designed an unusual variant apparently based upon the open legged all-in-ones worn by Chinese babies.

In 1977 Cardin launched a new venture 'pret-à-couture' for those who desired something between the exclusivity of haute couture and widely available pret-à-porter. *L'Officiel* praised him for this innovation and informed its readers that 'pret-à-couture' prices ranged from £200 to £400.

Between 1978 and 1980 the collections offered strictly tailored clothes alongside draped garments with softer lines. It is interesting to see short, tight black jersey *pantalons* worn under supple tunics drawn in by large cummerbunds and then slit at the sides from waist to hem. Cropped pants, first used by Cardin in 1960, were revived when it was considered appropriate. Their most recent appearance in black wool and lycra coincided with the 1980s youthful fad for bicycle shorts. By 1979 the tunics had shortened to loose tops bloused into low waists over tight black trousers tucked into high heeled boots. Another 1978 coup was a group of innocent-looking summer day-dresses, their fullness restrained over the breasts by crossed 'biblical' thongs. Evenings could be spent in long, cleverly cut and draped robes or in wilder creations such as a tiered mini dress over matching clinging trousers in a tree bark metallic fabric.

Returning from China in 1978, Cardin was inspired by its architecture and

decided that certain decorative elements could be included in sleeve construction. Initially he produced the pagoda sleeve with a distinctive upturned shoulder profile and continued inventing ever more ingenious sleeveheads. The range is enormous from diamond, heart and circle shapes to fanned epaulets and buttoned down petals. In some black leather blousons the sleeve tops resemble small pieces of sculpture and are remarkable technical achievements.

In 1979 the asymmetrical hemline was carried to its extreme in a number of powerful *tailleurs*. Over straight trousers, skirts dipped steeply from thigh length at one side to ankle length at the other, and were married to broad shouldered jackets. The look was re-inforced by aerodynamic felt cloches with brims slanted to echo the hemline.

For his autumn-winter collection 1982–3 Cardin was awarded the coveted De d'Or de la haute couture française (for the most creative collection of the season) by an international jury. This was his hat trick – he had received golden thimbles in 1977 and 1979. A portrait to commemorate this achievement shows Cardin in defiant mood balancing the three thimbles on an outstretched hand. He marked the beginning of the decade with work that defined yet another peak in his career.

Of particular note are a group of coats for winter 1980, in primary coloured wools with finned back panels (inspired by computer technology) which gently sway when their occupants walk. Like so many Cardin designs they challenge the divide between the applied and fine arts. They were photographed to great effect against the bright white architecture of then recently opened Forum des Halles. A shot of the couturier at work on a *toile* from this group indicates the complexity of their construction. Counterbalancing this tailored look are fun pieces including a youthful mini tube with hula hoop overskirt in spangled sherbet-coloured jersey. An amusing 'reversed roles' press photograph catches a young model eyeing two of the Elysée Palace guards patrolling avenue Marigny outside Cardin's boutiques. *L'Officiel* chose to take pictures of the mini dress in a circus ring where the unfortunate mannequin was compelled to pose alongside a performing elephant and dancing horse. The following year the press delighted in haute couture outfits for all the family based on an eminently practical combination of blouson and trousers or trouser suits. Sleeveless, in tweed or leather these have pronounced armholes with stiffened and top stitched edges curving up from the waist. Alternative designs have comical lobes attached to the shoulders.

The 1980s witnessed developments in two directions. The tailored collections became even stronger employing uncompromising and emphatic lines, while increasingly sumptuous extravaganzas were designed for evening wear. With a sure hand Cardin built upon past achievements yet without repetition or resorting to 'retro' continued to initiate over 300 designs for each season. When the time arrives to design the next collection Cardin and his team headed by André Oliver go into isolation until the demanding task is completed. These periods of intense creativity have to be fitted into a hectic time table involving worldwide personal visits.

Cardin received due acclaim in the early 1980s for his skill in manipulating cloth in smooth planes around the body. For distinctive day wear, white puritani-

cal collars extended from neck to waist where they were anchored with buttons. Summer dresses became two tubes split around the waist and held together by tabs at front and back. The geometry was continued in conical or domed hats and angular clutch bags. At night, sheath dresses in bold, plain colours were dramatised by huge volants or butterfly bows in crisp taffetas in contrasting hues. Frills and flounces play an important role in evening wear and are manipulated to gain maximum visual effect. The autumn-winter 1984–5 collection finished with two brides in identical gowns, one in white, the other in scarlet, comprised entirely of tiered ruffles. In 1985 *L'Officiel*, in an experiment to unite couture and fine art, commissioned the young artist Louis Lutz to sculpt three couture dresses including a slender draped gown by Cardin. The result was akin to a Grecian caryatid. In the same year Cardin strengthened his ties with China by inviting a party of girls to visit Paris and wear his designs. There were no professional Chinese models so Cardin's agent in China brought shop assistants and secretaries who provided ideal mannequins. Of the innumerable highlights between 1985 and 1990, the 1987 collections had a series of impressive winter capes with medieval overtones and the addition of winged helmets gave mannequins the look of ominous birds of prey. Less threatening suits had long jackets with deep belled cuffs and collars into which hands and faces could be demurely withdrawn. A much photographed black evening sheath had its back decorated with a vertical row of pleated pink satin fans each three feet wide. *Women's Wear Daily*, March 1988 was delighted with the short dresses on parade – 'The maddest of minis came from Pierre Cardin and André Oliver, who put together a marathon of minis Monday morning, adding up to a 350-piece collection that left the audience gasping for air'.

L'Officiel greeted Cardin's winter 1989–90 collection with the eulogy 'La créativité sans limites de Pierre Cardin' and went on to admire his almost arithmetical approach to volume and abstract form. He softened the asymmetry for which the house is well known and made huge coats that were short at the front and dipped along fluted lines to lower back hems. Each coat was topped by an immense fur hat which, being round or square, further emphasised the geometry underlying the collection. The beloved circles were revived for evening and, in red and black silk cloqué, skin-tight sheaths had skirts embellished with hooped overskirts. Most recently (spring-summer 1990) the grand coat theme was continued and clean cut, long line jackets in white and clear primaries were set over black toreador pants. In a different vein, plain black, white and purple ensembles had slender line tunic tops with prettily flared peplums. One work in particular – a purplish blue cape fanning out in pleats from neck to hem – interestingly brings to mind the pleated coats Pierre Cardin produced nearly forty years earlier. And thus the story comes full circle.

Much has been published about Pierre Cardin the product designer and business magnate. A recent profile counted 840 licences in 94 countries from America to the Soviet Union and detailed the ownership and expansion of Maxim and its offshoots. This shrewdly achieved empire underwrites that which is central to Pierre Cardin, couturier – the creative hubs of his theatre-gallery complex *Espace*

Cardin and, the subject of this pictorial survey – Pierre Cardin Haute Couture. With an almost museum-like precision, unusual in the pressurised world of fashion, Pierre Cardin has selected and kept examples from his couture collections dating back to the early 1950s. Combined with press cuttings and photographs from his archives, these originals give a unique picture of forty years of diverse and often provocative creation. It seems appropriate to conclude on a venture which linked the fine arts and the art of dress. In 1982, by invitation, Cardin showed a retrospective of haute couture at the Salon d'Automme. Considered by the members, eminent painters and sculptors, to be one of them he was introduced by the president Monsieur Mac Avoy – 'We painters and sculptors use canvas and marble for our creations whereas Pierre Cardin creates on living material . . .'.

Valerie Mendes

Biography

Pierre Cardin is French. He was born in Venice but grew up and was educated in France.

1945 Pierre Cardin comes to Paris. He works with Paquin and then Schiaparelli. He meets Jean Cocteau and Christian Bérard, with whom he starts designing masks and costumes for such movies as 'La Belle et La Bête'.

1947 Pierre Cardin joins Christian Dior who has just started his own company.

1950 Pierre Cardin forms his own fashion house.

1953 Pierre Cardin presents his first haute couture collection.

1954 Triumph of the bubble dress. Pierre Cardin opens his first boutique called 'Eve'.

1957 Pierre Cardin opens his second boutique called 'Adam', and was already planning a prêt-à-porter collection for men starting with 'fun' ties and patterned shirts.
First trip to Japan.

1958 Pierre Cardin is one of the judges for the Berkeley Debutante Dress Show in London.
Pierre Cardin is awarded 'Young Designer' by the town of Boston, USA.

1959 A coup within haute couture. Pierre Cardin is the first couturier to present a ready-to-wear collection for women, for which the Chambre Syndicale de la Couture expelled him. However, when other couturiers followed suit, he was soon welcomed back and subsequently elected President of the men's fashion division. Pierre Cardin signs his first licensing contract for men's shirts and ties; he creates exclusive design for *The Daily Telegraph*.

1960 Pierre Cardin shows his first ever men's collection using students as models.

1961 Opening of men's prêt-à-porter department.

1962 Creation of the Pierre Cardin prize, awarded to the best student of the year at 'Bunka Fu Kuso' school, Japan.

1963 Opening of women's ready-to-wear department.
Pierre Cardin is awarded *The Sunday Times* Oscar.
Pierre Cardin is awarded 'The Golden Spinning Wheel' in Krefeld, West Germany.

1965 First menswear show in the UK at the Savoy Hotel, London.

1966 Pierre Cardin shows his first children's collection.
Fashion show staged at The Commonwealth Institute, London.
Opening of Cardin Shop in Selfridges, London.

1968 Pierre Cardin opens a children's boutique just opposite 'Adam' and 'Eve'.

1970 Pierre Cardin opens the 'Espace Pierre Cardin', the theatre where Ella Fitzgerald, Shirley Bassey, and Marlene Dietrich amongst others have performed. The building also houses an art gallery, restaurant, and private cinema.

1973 Pierre Cardin is awarded the 'Basilica Palladiana', an award given every year to the most successful Venetian.

1974 Pierre Cardin is awarded the 'Eur Oscar', oscar of the Italian cinema given for his varied activities in the world of showbusiness.

1975 Opening of the first design boutique in Paris.

1976 Pierre Cardin receives the insignia of 'Commander of Order of Merit' from the Italian Republic.

1977 Pierre Cardin is awarded the 'Gold Thimble' for haute couture, an award given to the most creative designer of the season.
Pierre Cardin presents his first collection of avant garde furniture at the opening of the Gallery 'Evolution'.
Pierre Cardin opens his first 'Maxim's' boutique (food products and gifts).

1978 Pierre Cardin launches his furniture range in the UK.
Pierre Cardin is awarded the 'Prestige du Tourisme' certificate for his vital contribution to French tourism.
Launch of the first ready-to-wear for men, under the 'Maxim' label, with the opening of two boutiques in Paris.
First trip to China.

1979 Pierre Cardin is awarded the 'Gold Thimble' for the second time.
Pierre Cardin presents his collection for men and women in Peking and Shanghai.
Opening of the flower boutique 'Maxim's'.

1980 Pierre Cardin celebrates 30 years of design at the Metropolitan Museum and establishes his headquarters in New York.
Pierre Cardin opens his first shop in the Eastern Bloc in Sofia, Bulgaria.

1981 Pierre Cardin takes control of the famous Maxim's Restaurant, rue Royale, Paris.

Pierre Cardin is the first European designer to open a showroom in China, in Peking.

1982   Pierre Cardin presents 30 years of design including fashion, furniture and products at the Museum Sogetsu Kakain, Tokyo.
Pierre Cardin is awarded the 'Gold Thimble' for the third time.

1983   Opening of the 'Minim's' restaurant in Paris.
Pierre Cardin is invited to show his designs and products in Moscow.
'Maxim's' restaurants open in Peking and Rio de Janeiro.
Pierre Cardin receives the insignia of 'Chevalier de l'Ordre des Arts et des Lettres'.

1984   London boutique is launched at 20 Old Bond Street.
Opening of 'Minim's' restaurant in Peking.

1985   Pierre Cardin receives the insignia of 'Commandeur de l'Ordre National du Mérite' from the President of the French Republic.
Maxim's restaurant opens in New York.
Launch of the first perfume 'Maxim's' for women.

Pierre Cardin receives the 'Oscar de la Mode' at the Paris Opera.

1986   Licensing agreement signed with USSR for the manufacture of ready-to-wear clothing for men, women, and children.
The opening of Hôtel 'Résidence Maxim's' in Paris.

1987   The decoration of the Grande Ufficiale is conferred on Pierre Cardin by the Italian Republic.

1988   Launch of 'Maxim's' fragrance for men.

1989   Major haute couture presentations in Pakistan, India, Australia, Spain, Italy, and Denmark.

1990   *Pierre Cardin: past, present, future.* A retrospective exhibition at the Victoria & Albert Museum, London, 10 October 1990 – 6 January 1991.

1 *1951*

19 51

2 1951

3 1952

1953

6 1956

7 1956

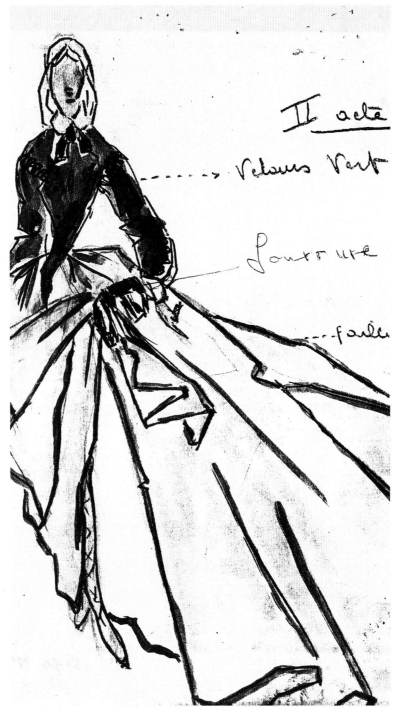

II acte

Velours Vert

fourrure

faille

9 *1950*

10 *1957*

11 *1957*

12 *1958*

13 *1958*

14 *1958*

15 *1959*

16 *1960*

17 1960

19 *1963*

20 *1964*

21 *1964*

23 1966

24 *1966*

25 *1966*

40

26 1965

27 1965

28 1966

29 1966

30 1966

43

31 1966

ESPACE
PIERRE CARDIN

32 1966

34 *1966*

35 *1966*

37 1966

42 *1969*

43 *1968*

44 *1968*

46 *1968*

47 *1968*

48 *1968*

49 *1968*

51 *1968*

52 *1968*

54 1969

55 1969

56 *1969*

59 *1969*

Gloves 1970–71

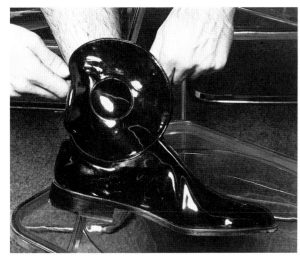
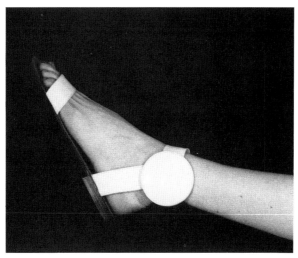

Head and footwear 1966–71

61 1969

62 1969

63 1969

65 *1970*

66 *1970*

67 1970

68 *1970*

70 *1970*

71 *1970*

73 1970

74 1970

75 1970

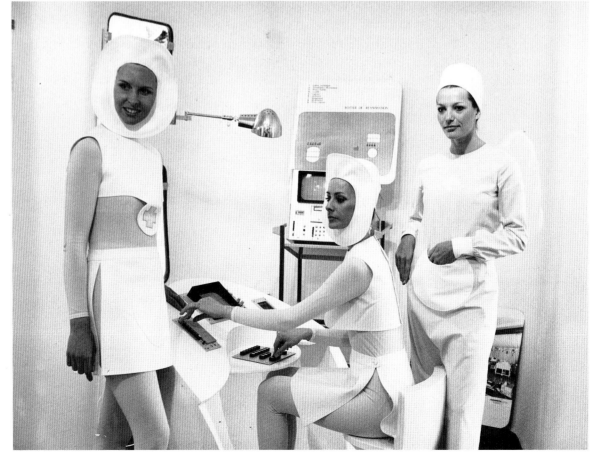

76 1970

77 1971

78 1971

80 *1971*　　　　　81 *1971*　　　　　82 *1971*

85 *1971*

Espace Pierre Cardin

Cinema

Theatre

Exterior

Restaurant

Fashion glasses 1971–72

86 *1971*

87 1971

89 *1971*

90 *1971*

91 *1972*

92 *1972*

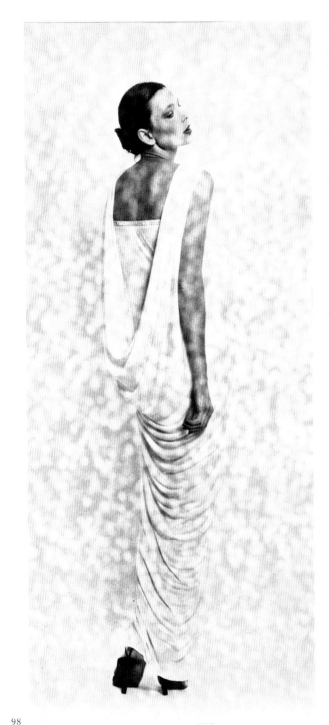

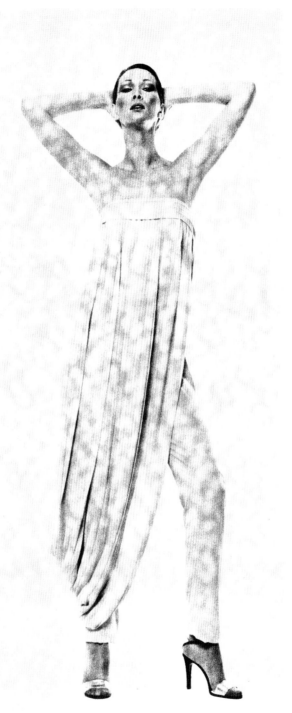

93 *1975*

94 *1975*

95 *1975*

96 1974

97 1974

99 *1974*

100 *1974*

101 *1977*

102 *1977*

103 *1977*

104 *1977*

105 *1977*

108 *1977*

109 *1978*

110 *1978*

112 *1978*

113 *1978*

115 *1979*

116 *1979*

Furniture

 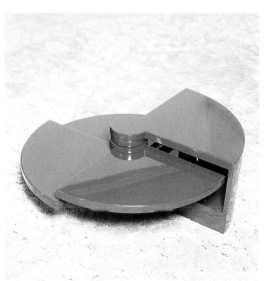

113

Furniture

114

122 *1980*

123 *1980*

126 *1980*

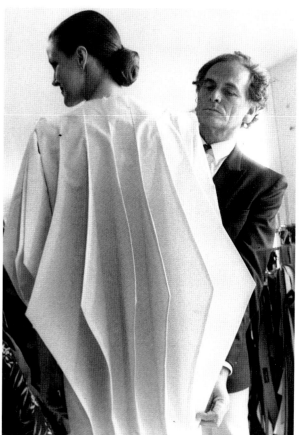

127 *1980*

128 *1980*

129 *1980*

130 *1982*

131 *1980*

132 *1981*

124

133 *1981*

136 *1981*

137 *1981*

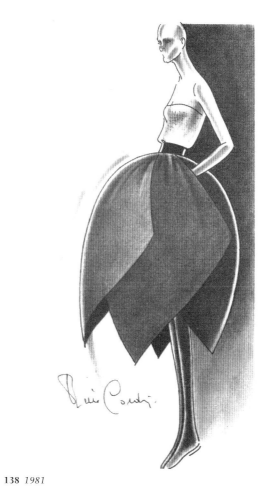

138 *1981*

139 *1981*

140 *1981*

141 *1981*

127

142 *1981*

143 *1981*

144 *1981*

145 *1982*

146 *1982*

146a

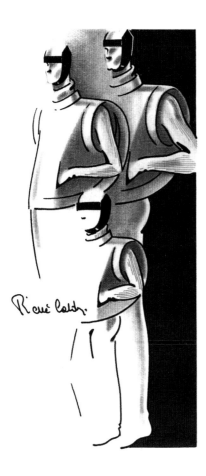

147a

147 *1982*

133

150 *1982*

151 *1982*

152 *1982*

153 *1982*

154 *1982*

155 *1982*

156 *1982*

157 *1982*

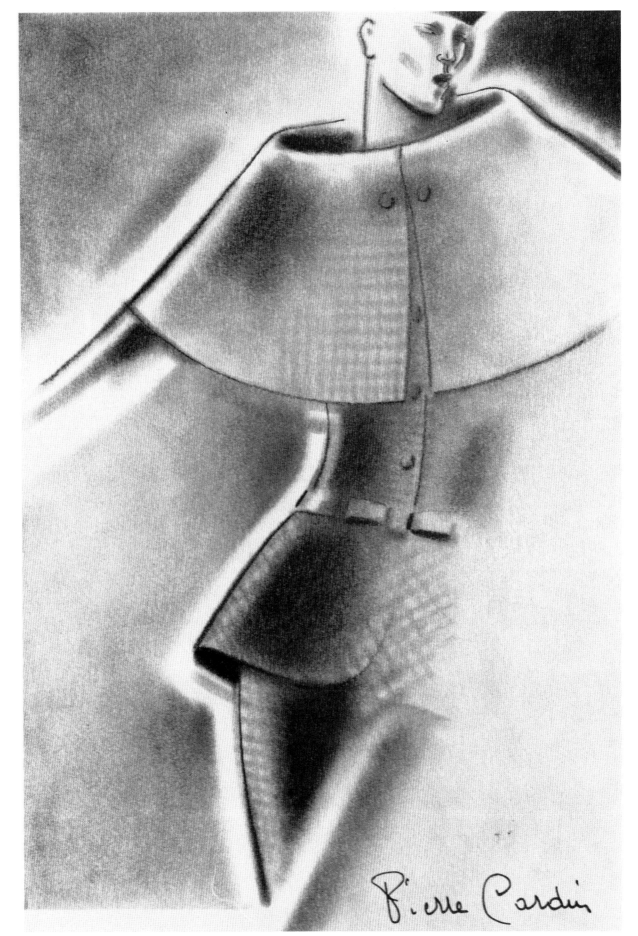

159 *1982*

140

160 *1983*

161 *1982*

162 *1983*

163 *1983*

164 *1984*

165 1984

166 *1983*

167 *1984*

168 *1984*

169 *1985*

170 *1985*

171 *1985*

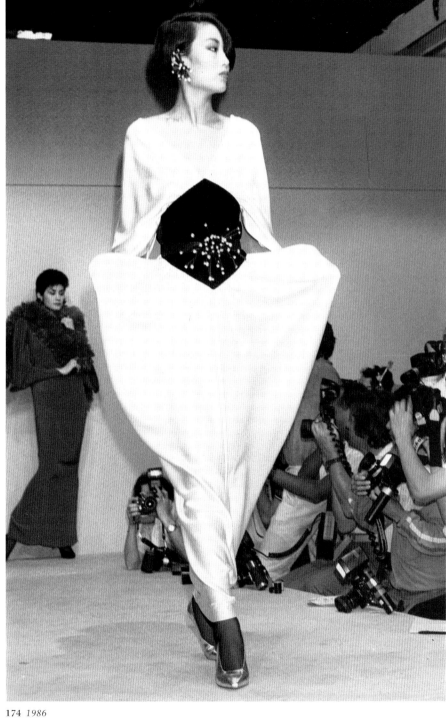

174 *1986*

175 *1987*

153

178 *1986*

154

179 *1986*

180 *1986*

181 *1987*

183 *1986*

184 *1987*

185 *1987*

186 *1987*

189 *1988*

190 *1988*

193 *1989*

194 *1989*

169

197 *1989*

198 *1989*

199 *1989*

200 *1990*

201 *1989*

202 *1989*

203 *1990*

205 1990

206 *1990*

207 *1990*

208 *1990*

209 *1990*

211 *1990*

212 *1990*

184

Autumn/Winter 1990–91

185

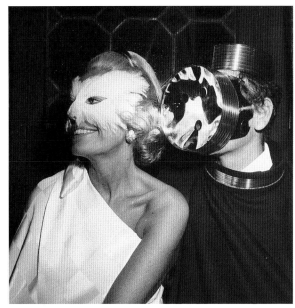

The publishers are aware that the quality of reproduction of images is not one-hundred per cent uniform.

Some shots were taken on the catwalk at the haute couture shows, giving a refreshing feel of intimacy with other press photographers in view rather than shots of specially-posed models.

Using a printed page or a copy print for artwork inevitably leads to a variation in definition; unfortunately negatives or original prints are no longer extant for some photographs and therefore this was the only method of reproducing such material.